Raymond D. Johnson

Out of the Frying Pan and Into the Fire

Redding Fire Publishing

Table of Contents

Chapter One

FIRST 18 YEARS – I was adopted from birth by Roy and Ruth Johnson. I was their second child, Warren 1 ½ years older was their first adopted son. We lived on a farm in Maple Valley, Washington State during the first couple of years. I remember that a fire occurred in the kitchen of this house when I was a young child and recall taking a toy bucket, dipping it in the toilet and helping mom put the fire out. I never knew if this influenced my future fire service career or ever knew how this fire started. We moved from there in the early 60's to a large white house at 22426 30th Avenue

South, Des Moines, Washington. Our family had a large piece of property and a lot of kids in the neighborhood came over. I remember Renee and Randy Carroll, Emmett Heath and his sisters, Mike Fryrear, Kathy Kasper, Cheri and Dusty Humes, Sgt Don Obermiller, and Rick Harding. From 1962 – 1966 my brother Warren and I helped our dad build ten cottages (small homes for rent). The rentals went well. During this time, a large shop/Apartment was built next to the big house and later burned to the ground in late 1966. During the years of 1966 and 1967 my adopted parents started going out more and more. They would either leave us alone on the nights they could not find a babysitter, or we would be looked after by one of several girls that my parents used. This was the year that one of the babysitters raped both Warren and me. (I could go into detail here as needed) For the next several years, I had nightmares of monsters climbing up to our window (second floor) and trying to get us. I started wetting the bed, snuck out on the weekends, and was required to pee in a pot upstairs because we did not have a toilet upstairs. I was always the one who had to empty and clean the pot every day. I started drinking during these years. I was considered a fat child and Warren and his friends used to taunt me daily. We had moved four houses south on 30th avenue during this time. My parents were gone every night of the week during this time in my life. They used to leave money on the table for "dinner" each night. Not only did they drink more but both Warren and I started drinking as much as we could get our hands on. I remember a large oak tree in the back half of the property, and I would hide there often, up in the branches, away from the crazy world I was living in. One night Roy came home and mistook my snare drum for the toilet. He peed all over the drum. The next morning, I threw the drum away and never played the drum again. One time I was at a friend's house in Midway, WA, at 30th Avenue and Kent Des Moines Road. I was upstairs with one of the kids when we heard a gunshot in the house. As we went downstairs, we discovered my friend had accidentally been shot by another youngster in the house. I ran to a nearby fire station and got help. They got there and carried my friend out on a door. I could tell he was dead as he was doing the death shutter (convulsing) while being carried out. Later when I got home no one was there. Mom and Dad were at the Midway tavern. I called there and asked them to come home so I could talk to them. They said they would, but they did not get home until after midnight and we never spoke about the death.

In 1968, I had my spleen and appendix removed after spending six months in the University of Washington Hospital. I had the symptoms of hemophiliac and would bruise easily, and a small cut would bleed profusely. My spleen was found to be diseased and once it was removed, my physical ailments went away. Later that year, I got hit by a speeding car that I turned into while riding my bike. I sustained a broken left leg and a serious concussion. I stayed in the hospital for another week and 10 weeks of recovery. I was lucky this happened after my surgery as I would have probably bled to death if it had occurred before the splenectomy.

We played a lot of war games during these years. The small forest in the back of the property got dark even during the day. I was very scared of the dark and still struggle today with being slightly claustrophobic and scared of the dark. We were in this house for about 10 years. For the first 6 years I was taunted daily by my brother and his friends. I finally started wrestling in Junior High School and started fighting back. After a couple of hard-fought battles, I was finally left alone by them, not accepted by them but at least left alone. I was working as a volunteer at the local grocery store (Tradewell Stores) in Midway and at 16 was hired by them as a store grocery bagger. I stayed there for about 6 months and left due to not having enough work hours a week. Shortly after that I started working for Sambo's Restaurants' and worked for them for 3 years. During this time, I moved out of my parent's home due to the constant abuse and alcoholism. I rented an apartment with my best friend at the time, Randy Locke. I continued to go to high school during this time and slid under the school's rules for several months. It was not uncommon for me to wake up in the dark and not know whether it was day or night. I was either working, going to school or sleeping. I moved back in with Roy and Ruth for a brief period to time the later part of my junior year and the summer between that year and my senior year. The drinking and associated activity was worse than ever. I only stayed as long as I could stand it and get enough money to move out again. I than rented an apartment above my girlfriend, Roene Caldwell and her mother, June. During this time, the school caught up with me and I had to go in front of a review board to decide if my living arrangement met the rules and laws. I was 17 and a senior at the time. My mother, Roene's mother and I went in front of a district review board. I had to tell them about my parent's alcoholism and my living arrangement. They ruled that June Caldwell could act as my guardian for the rest of my senior year. I was also allowed to sign my own sick slips that

the school required when returning from
illness. That turned out to be quite a joke
with the school. As I finished high school,
I continued to work at Sambo's, then
the West Seattle Steak House and as a
carpet installer. My parents quick claimed
deeded a home to me. The bank was
going to repossess the home because
Roy was behind in his payments. He
and the bank struck a deal to refinance
the original loan ($13,500) and deed
it over to me. For the first two years, I
made payments to the bank through
Roy. The bank finally gave me the loan
as I was more conscientious than Roy
was with the loan. I later sold that home
for $92,000 to the Port of Seattle due
to the location of the home in relation
to the south end of Seattle International
Airport. I acquired the home in 1974, the

same year I graduated from Tyee High School on South 188th. After graduation I stumbled around for a couple of years, wondering what life had in store for me.

Chapter Two
Early Fire Service

I took the Seattle Fire Department's test and came out 313 out of 1000 applicants. I thought that was rather good but did not want to wait to get called from them. This was during the time of affirmative action, and I found out later that a lot of people of color or females' way past the number I was on the list were getting hired. I found a fire department to volunteer for about this time.

THE START OF MY FIRE SERVICE CAREER:

In the summer of 1976, I walked into King County Fire District #26 in Des Moines,

Washington. I spoke to the first person I saw in an office and asked him (turned out to be the Fire Chief) if they needed volunteers. He said they did. He told me to shave my beard off, get my hair cut and come back that night. I went home, shaved my beard, but did not have time for a haircut. That evening I returned to the fire station for drill. I had tucked my long hair up under my hat. I was given all the gear for getting started and was told of a training burn two Saturdays away. My picture was in the local newspaper during that training burn and I was stuck in the fire service for life. Being a firefighter came easily for me and the socialization with the other guys and two gals was just what I needed. I was accepted and met some of the finest people in the world while at KCFD #26. One of those people

was Ron Biesold. He came walking in
one day and had just gotten home from
the service. He became my roommate
and we have been best friends for the
past 40 years. Some of the more unique
and terrifying calls I went on are while a
volunteer with KCFD #26 were:

King County Fire District #26
Group Photo

One of the first house fires I went on was at 7th and 223rd. I was directed to vent the roof. I was up on the roof, no roof ladder, no self-contained breathing apparatus, and with limited experience. The roof vented with the first swipe of the axe, and I had 20-foot flames dancing all around me. I remember scrambling off the roof and falling the last ten feet to the ground. I was not hurt too badly but I was shaken up.

We had a house fire at 10th and 224th. The back room was on fire and the fire was already venting through an open back door. It was dark and raining. As I was approaching the house, trying to get my gear on properly, I stumbled

and fell to the ground. Ron Biesold
picked me up and he and I went
side by side into the doorway of this
home. The fire was all around us
and extremely hot. I was trying to
back out and Ron kept me in place
and pointed to where he wanted
me to direct the hose line. This
experience was unnerving as I was
trying to get my emotions under
control and put this fire out or at
least knock it down. The physical
exertion of extinguishing a fire is one
of the most extreme anyone could
ever endure. You must learn through
experience to control your breathing,
your fight or flight syndrome, the
pacing of your strength and your
wanting to raise the level of pitch in
your voice during an emergency. It

took me several years to do this and even at the end of my career it was all I could do not to scream for help in the middle of an emergency.

One of the most unique and scary calls during my volunteer time at KCFD #26 was an auto accident at Saltwater State Park. A car with four or five young people in it was leaving the park at a high rate of speed. The driver got distracted and veered right at the open gate to the right. The gate went into the windshield and all the way into the back seat. When we got there, we had several injured patients, but the driver was missing. As we extricated the patients from the car, we learned the driver was on a bridge nearby threatening to jump.

(He thought he had killed everyone
in the car during the accident) As
I approached the driver, he had
one leg over the bridge and was
threatening to jump. The distance to
the ground was about 200 feet and
a fall from this height would certainly
be fatal. I attempted to calm the
driver and tell him everyone was
going to be ok. He was intoxicated
and did not believe me. As I was
talking to him, I was edging closer to
his location. When I was about ten
feet away, he took his eyes off of me
and looked down from the bridge.
I grabbed the leg still on this side
of the bridge and did not let go. He
attempted to jump but I did not let go
and we ultimately got him back on
the roadway. WOW, what a call.

We did CPR a lot when we were at KCFD #26. We had a large number of nursing homes in our community. Do not resuscitate laws were not in affect yet so we tried to save everyone. King County Medic One was just coming into existence and we were learning emergency medicine as we were going along trying our best to save people.

Pacific Highway South (Hwy 99) ran right though out district, and we ran on a lot of automobile accidents. Many of them were minor but some required some very technical rescues while trying not to injure the patient further while trying to get them out of the vehicle.

One night we were dispatched to a

motorcycle accident on Marine View Drive. When we arrived, we found a single patient in critical condition. He had slid into a concrete barrier and had a terrible head injury. Several months later we saw this same man in a nursing home. He had been in a coma since the accident. He was in this nursing home for several years and every time we saw him, he had deteriorated more and more. He had a young daughter at the time of the accident, and we watched her grow up while her father suffered for years.

Another motorcycle accident we were sent to was just north of Des Moines. A biker had been traveling at a high rate of speed and as he came around a corner, he sideswiped a bus. He had a compound fracture of his left femur and was conscious during our treatment. His main concern was that we did not cut off his boot or his leather pants. He was adamant that we did not cut off his clothes. We ended up cutting the laces to the boot and then up the seam of his leather pants. We then applied a temporary splint to his left leg and transported him to the hospital.

During this time of my volunteer service came a ton of training. I completed several courses in basic firefighter and became good at hose evolutions. I was chosen as one of the team members for our hose evolution team and competed with them for about four years. We won several competitions during this time. I still have some of the trophies now thirty years later. My girlfriend during this time was Bev Schalow. She was a tall blond girl and we at one time were engaged to be married. In 1978, when she found out that I was going to be a full-time police officer with Hoquiam, WA she threw the engagement ring at me and told me to get out. (I wonder what happened to her?)

Chapter Three
Reserve Law Enforcement

In 1977, at the encouragement of then Sgt. Don Obermiller, I joined the Des Moines Reserve Academy. Law enforcement came extremely easy for me and after six weeks of training, two nights a week and Saturdays, we graduated. I was the top in my class and felt proud of that accomplishment. During my time at Des Moines, we had some interesting calls:

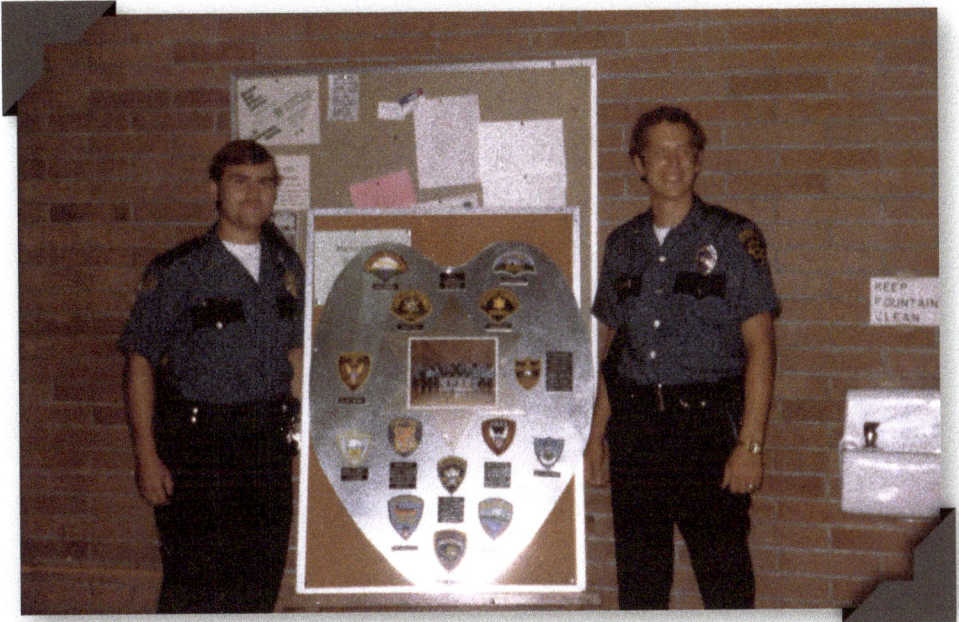

Reserve Police Graduation

Sgt. Obermiller and I rode together
a lot and one night we got a call of
a silent alarm at one of the retail
dress shops in town. We checked
the street front door and found it
locked. When we went around back
we found a downstairs door open.
We entered and with guns drawn
searching for bad guys. At one point

I saw a shadow of a person in the corner and yelled "freeze." Well, that got Obermiller's attention, and he came to see what I had captured. When we shined our lights on the shadow, with adrenaline flowing and our guns drawn, it turned out to be a naked manikin. Lucky for me I did not shoot the manikin. I would never have lived it down.

During this time in our culture the Black Panthers were robbing banks. They were extremely violent and would often set up ambushes for the responding police officers. At that time in law enforcement, especially small towns like Des Moines, the only weapons we carried were handguns and shotguns. The

Panthers were carrying assault rifles and sophisticated automatics. One of the Des Moines Police officers came from military training and was allowed to secretly carry an automatic weapon. The secrecy of this was especially important. If the word got out who was carrying the "big" gun, we would have been targeted as soon as we got on scene. I remember this officer showing me this weapon one night and gave me a quick lesson on its workings and how to shoot it.

During my time as a Reserve Police Officer, I worked weekends as security for the Des Moines Marina. One Saturday I was walking along the pier. Homes and apartments dotted the bluff across the parking lot. I looked up to one of the apartments and a young woman was dancing in the plate glass window. She was in full view of the parking lot and was nude. I stopped for several minutes watching this erotic expedition. Then it dawned on me that I was standing there in a police uniform watching this young lady dancing nude in front of me and for the entire world to see. I moved on down the pier and left her behind. Later I reported what I saw to Sgt. Obermiller and we had a good laugh about it. I thought about going back off duty and introducing myself, but never did.

One night we were on patrol on

Pacific Hwy South and ran a plate/ vehicle for wants and warrants. As it turned out the occupants of this vehicle had felony warrants for their arrest. We followed the vehicle southbound on PHS until we had several police units as back up. We executed a felony stop in the middle of PHS. The four occupants were removed from their vehicle. All four lanes of the highway were closed for approximately fifteen minutes as this process unfolded. I remember the excitement of the moment. I was totally focused on the process and the safety of the officers involved. I remember, as the scene started to cool down, looking over at some of the innocent bystanders stuck in traffic. I saw the terror and excitement in their faces and wondered what they thought of the whole ordeal. Once the bad guys were secured, their vehicle properly searched, we reopened the highway and the bystanders got out of there quickly. It is so much different now as there are many police shows, true crime and reality pursuits, that most people take these scenarios as common place unless they are victims of the crimes. Even then, a lot of the victims feel like it is supposed to be common for them to be involved. Today there are cell phones and body cameras that capture events in real time. We did not have that in my day, for which I am thankful.

While a Reserve, I also worked as a police dispatcher for Des Moines.

I typically worked the graveyard shift, 11 to 7. During my stint as a dispatcher, I had some interesting and terrifying calls:

One warm night at about 2:30 am I had the front door of the station propped open. These were the days before bullet proof glass, or any partitions between the public and the dispatcher, other than a counter. I was sitting behind my dispatch desk and directly outside the door, on South 223rd came two very loud shotgun blasts. I was stunned for about 30 seconds, collected my breath and as calm, cool and collected as possible stated, "S-10, dispatch, shots fired at the station."

Sgt. Obermiller came onto the air and stated, "SHOTS FIRED?" I stated, "Affirmative." That brought all units to the station as quickly as possible. We had two out that night. Of course, I could not give a description of the suspect vehicle because I was under the desk trying to hide as much as possible. We never did know who fired the shots but did find shotgun pellets in the side of the station.

Another night I took a phone call from a homeowner on Pacific Hwy South. He had found a burglar in his home after returning to it. He had the suspect cornered in his house and was pointing a handgun at him. I learned that this call was in King

County Sheriff's jurisdiction and
called County Dispatch. As I was
relating the call to that dispatch,
I was yelling at the homeowner
to NOT shoot the suspect. The
homeowner was yelling at the
suspect that he was going to shot
him if he moved. Thank God the
suspect did not move. This was
a very tense situation for about 5
minutes until the county police got
to the scene and apprehended the
suspect. When I got off the phone,
I was shaking, and it took several
minutes to calm down. I made a
notation in the dispatch logbook and
went on about my work.

Chapter Four
Law Enforcement Career

During all this time I was testing for police and fire jobs. I came remarkably close to being hired at the Bellevue Fire Department. I was interviewed as one of the top five candidates for a job, was told I had the job and then told the next day that the candidate who interviewed behind me got the job. I also tested and was offered a position with the Seattle/ Tacoma Airport fire department. During this time, I tested and got hired by the Hoquiam, WA Police Department. I made the decision to take the Hoquiam job. I moved to Hoquiam and began my career as a full-time police officer. For two or three months I was allowed on the street without going to the Washington State Police Academy because I had been a reserve officer in Des Moines. I rode with Officer Don Burke, a 10-year veteran of the Hoquiam and Raymond, WA police departments. Don had a great family; a wife and three little girls. Working graveyard was tough for him as he did not get much sleep during the day. It was common to find him dosing off in the quite early morning hours of this small-town police work. One of the most memorable calls of my early time at Hoquiam was a domestic violence call.

One evening we were on the east side of town getting coffee and donuts in an all-night "stop and rob." In walks a female who looked beaten pretty badly. This was long before the domestic violence laws came into effect, and we had a lot of discretion about how we managed the situations to which we were called. At a minimum, this was an assault and battery case that needed follow-up. Officer Burke took the lead and asked her if she wanted to press charges. She told us all she wanted to do was get to her car and leave, no charges, no problems. We drove her to her house and as she was trying to get into her car, which was parked directly in front of her home on the street, here came the husband. He came storming out of the house, obviously intoxicated. He stood up on the porch and began screaming at the wife not to take the car. Officer Burke was in between the husband and the wife, on the sidewalk. I was positioned off to the left of Officer Burke approximately 6 feet away. A slight drizzle of rain had begun to fall. During all the yelling back and forth, the husband stated he would get his gun, and nobody would be taking anything anywhere. A couple of seconds later, the husband reached under his open shirt and pulled out a handgun. He pointed it directly at the wife and Officer Burke. I drew my weapon and ordered the husband to drop his gun. I was yelling loudly and could feel myself starting to put pressure on the trigger of my weapon. Out of my peripheral vision I could see that Officer Burke was standing there, no gun drawn, no action, just standing there in the rain. I yelled again for the husband to put down his gun. Everything slowed to a crawl. It was like slow motion however I knew all of this would be over in a few seconds. The husband looked at me, looked at his wife and looked back at me. He then pointed the gun into the air and cocked it, (pulled back the hammer). I could see directly behind the husband, his children crying from inside the house. They were in my line of fire and for a fleeting moment I was concerned for them seeing their father get killed by me. I yelled one more time. The husband then moved the gun towards me, cocked. I continued to pull on the trigger and knew that in ½ more pound of pressure I would be killing this man. In that instant he dropped the gun on the ground. I released my pressure on the trigger and the hammer of my weapon released slowly back in its safe position.

We approached the husband and secured him. I took custody of his weapon. We told the wife to leave, and she drove off. Officer Burke then took control of the scene, and after emptying the bullets from the gun gave it back to the husband. Officer Burke left the husband at the scene and if my memory is correct, did minimal paperwork to document this call. I on the other hand shook for the better part of an hour. I had only been in Hoquiam for about three weeks and had been put through this situation. I collected myself, cleared the scene and went for a drive. When I returned to the station at approximately 5 am, Officer Burke had already told the story of what a fantastic job I did. I never told the story of how Officer Burke did not draw his weapon during this situation that obviously required us to protect ourselves and the wife.

Hoquiam was known for its population of American Indians and Loggers. It was typical that these two factions did not get along. They were both hard workers and hard drinkers. One night we got a call of a large fight in progress at a local night club. As this was my patrol area, I was closest. I got there and as I looked into the side entrance saw about a dozen men fighting. I called for back-up and stood in the door. As one of the fighters got close to me, I grabbed him and threw him out the door. I did this about five or six times and the guys inside realized that the fight was beginning to end. By that time, my back up had arrived and unbeknownst to the fighters inside were taking the guys outside into custody. As the fight was winding down, we entered and took the rest of the combatants into custody. As it turns out I got a little bit of a reputation for handling this incident by myself. I did have lots of help though; the other officers were all outside taking care of business there.

I participated in a few pursuits during my time at Hoquiam. One of them was a slow pursuit of a DUI driver bouncing from the east bound bridge over the Hoquiam River. When he finally stopped, I called for back-up and got out to interview the driver and confirm his ability to drive or not to drive. I asked him to exit the vehicle and to perform several field sobriety tests. He failed these tests and as I attempted to take him into custody found him to be quite a bit stronger than me. He spun me around and threw me to the ground landing on top of me. He was punching my face and I was trying to find my weapon. As I was face down on the ground, if I could have found my weapon, I would have had

to reach around my left ear to shoot
this guy off me. My weapon was not
in its holster, damn. Suddenly, as I
started to lose consciousness, I felt
the bad guy start to let go. I did a
push up with all the strength I had
left and a good rush of adrenaline
and was standing facing this guy
and my back-up officer. We secured
this combatant and literally threw
him into the back seat of a patrol car.
As it turns out I was a bloody mess.
Cuts and bruises on my face and
arms. A few minutes later a citizen
walked up to me with my weapon
in his hand and asked me if it was
mine. He had found it in the grass
directly beneath me where I was
lying down getting the crap beat out
of me.

Chapter Five

While at the Hoquiam Police Department, Washington State Law mandated me to attend the state police academy in South Seattle, WA. The academy was located at the south end of Seattle/Tacoma International Airport. It was eleven weeks long, was very intense and very physically challenging. In my academy class were a number of Kent, WA police officers. We became close friends and during the academy I took the Kent Police Department exam. I scored well enough to get hired and started there shortly after the academy ended. Within four months of leaving Hoquiam and moving back to south Seattle to work at Kent PD, Hoquiam Officer Don Burke was killed in the line of duty while pursuing two bank robbers. The story goes that he spotted the robbers and took up a high-speed pursuit. As he came around a corner the robber's vehicle had spun out and was facing him. The bad guy in the passenger seat got out and approached Officer Burke who was calling in his position to dispatch. The robber fired several shots into Officer Burke. Officer Burke got out of his vehicle, returned fire, reloaded, and emptied his weapon one more time before dying on the ground behind his patrol vehicle. He died a hero's death, giving his life to protect the public from these two ruthless men. The two robbers were later killed in one of the most dramatic shoot outs in Grays Harbor history by several

law enforcement agencies that had
caught up to them east of Aberdeen, WA.
I read this story at breakfast the morning
after it happened in the local Kent paper.
The name of the officer was omitted but
somehow, I knew who it was. I made
a phone call to Hoquiam and my worst
fears were realized. Kent Police Chief
Jay Skewes and I went to the funeral. It
was one of the toughest and most difficult
days of my life. Seeing the pain and
suffering Officer Burke's little girls were
going through and would go through for
the rest of their lives was heart wrenching
for me.

Chapter Six

I was an officer with the Kent Police
Department for five years from 1979 –
1984. These years were crazy for the
city, the community at large and the
department. The city was growing by an
astronomical amount of people which
equated into a huge increase in calls for
service and crimes committed. I met and
married my wife during these years. The
Green River Killer started his killing spree
in 1982. My original field training officer
was John Fletcher. He was a big, growly
guy who as it turns out was really a big
teddy bear. He later shot and killed the
driver of a felony stopped vehicle when

his weapon accidently discharged. Some of my most memorable calls <u>while I was on patrol</u> were:

Chapter Seven

An attempt to locate was put out by dispatch for a young mental patient who was late coming back to the institution from an outing. He was described as 5'9" slim build with a Santa Claus suit on. Within fifteen minutes I spotted this fellow on South 240th and gave him a ride back to his "home". A few weeks later we got a similar call that this person was again late and of course I was the officer that found him. As I approached him, he started to run from me. I called for back-up, caught up with the guy and placed him up against a nearby wall. He started to resist and as I was explaining to him the ramifications of resisting apprehension, my microphone on my radio was active. All the officers on the street at the time heard my warnings and the command-and-control tone in my voice. Suddenly, I had three other patrol cars around me with several police officers assisting me in placing this fellow in custody. When one of the officers asked me what this "suspect" was under arrest for I told him that he was not under arrest for anything. It took a very few minutes for the assisting officers to clear out and leave me with transporting Santa Claus back to his institution. From then on, I was known as the officer who arrested Santa Claus.

Over the period of several evening shifts we were continually dispatched to a home in southeastern Kent where a lady had a restraining order against her husband. By the time we got there the husband was always gone. We decided one night to stake out the residence to see if we could apprehend the husband. The wife was really scared of him and was concerned we were not doing enough to keep him away from her. I was positioned down a dark street in my patrol car and my senior partner, Jim Miller, was up on the roof of the wife's home. After about a half hour a male person comes walking up the walkway towards the house. My partner notified me by radio that the suspect was there and that I should move up. As I did and got to the front of the house, I saw my partner jump from the roof onto the husband. As it turns out, the husband was leaving a large Easter bunny and some candy for the wife for Easter. We took the husband into custody for violation of the restraining order and of course got a lot of ribbing from our fellow officers about arresting the Easter bunny. This plus the Santa Claus incident made us infamous.

Late one swing shift evening an officer reported that he had been shot. The location of the shooting was on the Green River Road approximately one mile north of the Green River Bridge. A suspect description was given out and graveyard shift officers were called in. I was one of the graveyard officers and was positioned halfway up Kent Des Moines Road for most of the night. I was armed with a shot gun and service revolver but due to the nature of the call and number of officers; I had no vehicle to keep warm in. I did have a radio for communications.

This was one of the longest nights I have ever spent. I heard noises in the bushes and thought the bad guys were going to shoot me too. Every time a vehicle came up Kent Des Moines Road, I would hide on the side of the road just in case it was the suspects. As it turns out, after a complete investigation, this officer faked his own shooting. He was released from employment due to psychiatric problems and we later found out he had relocated to a gated community in Texas and was a security officer there. He lost that job when they found out his background.

One day I was on patrol in the downtown district and got a call of a possible deceased person in an upstairs apartment. As I went up the stairs a terrible odor met me. Once you have smelled a dead body, you never forget that smell. I opened the door to the apartment and saw a large man lying on the bed obviously deceased. The odor was so bad I called the fire department to bring me a SCBA (self-contained breathing apparatus). This piece of equipment allowed someone to breath in a toxic environment. Due to my fire department background, I was allowed to use this equipment to conduct my initial investigation of this man's death. After about an hour, I called the medical examiner and exited the apartment. Returning the breathing equipment to the fire department allowed me to complete the scene exam from the exterior of the building. It turns out that the extreme odor had permeated my clothes and I stunk for the rest of my shift. It took several washings to extract the odor from my uniform.

Late one night we received a call of a silent alarm from a supply store on Central Avenue south. As we arrived, we formed a perimeter around the exterior of a large fenced in outdoor storage area. My FTO (Field Training Officer) directed me to climb the fence in order to search inside. I climbed the ten-foot fence and as I placed one leg over both of my feet lost their grips. I landed on the barb wire with my crotch and let out a painful scream. At that point I felt like I was at shooting gallery stuck on the fence for anyone to knock me off. Luckily no one was in the storage area and the only loss I had was a new pair of uniform pants and very little physical damage. I did take a lot of ribbing from my teammates though.

One swing shift (3pm till 11 pm) I was assigned to the downtown district. At this time the Kent Police Department did not have any detectives. Once a patrol officer received a call for service, they were expected to follow through with the investigation no matter where it took them. On this particular day I was dispatched to a call at the department headquarters. Once there I met two young woman who wanted to report that the younger one had been sexually abused by her father for a number of years. I began a lengthy investigation that took several days. During this time, I learned that the abuser was a Deputy Fire Chief for the local fire department. He had been in psychological therapy for a period of time for his behavior. This therapy had been mandated by a family court as long as he was married. He was soon to be divorced and the therapy would stop. His daughters were concerned that he would continue his actions after the divorce. Due to the political nature of the abusers position I confided with my Sergeant, my Captain, and the Chief of Police. We set up a false meeting with the abuser in the Police Chief's office. During the course of the investigation, we learned that the abuser was known to be armed and had threatened to kill himself if any of his actions got out in the open. We did notify the Fire Chief in confidence, so he was not taken by surprise. On the day of the false meeting, I had two extra officers standing by outside of the meeting room. The abuser came in and sat down across the table from me. I asked him if he was armed, and he stated he was not. I did a quick frisk of him to confirm, he was not. I began by reading him his constitutional rights. He asked me what this was all about, and I explained that one of his daughters had made a complaint that he had sexually abused her for the past eleven years. He told me that I was wrong, it had only been seven years. I was shocked by him spontaneously admitting to this crime. He asked me what he should do. I told him he should seek the advice of an attorney. Luckily, I had recorded his confession. I arrested him and booked him into our jail. He ended up at Western State Hospital for a mental breakdown and retired soon thereafter. The last I heard of him was he had a job putting up billboard posters.

One late swing shift, I was assigned to the industrial district. I observed a speeding motorcycle run a red light and gave chase. He led me on a five-mile-high speed chase up 212th street. As we got to a right-hand turn, he turned left through the woods. During this chase I learned that one of my backup officers was involved in a crash as he was responding to assist me. I lost the motorcycle and got stuck on the wooded trail. Due to the adrenaline rush I exited my patrol car and attempted to "chop" down a nearby tree with my nightstick. Luckily, the backup officer wasn't terribly injured but I was still determined to locate the motorcycle. I never did but heard rumors later that the person riding the bike was well known to the fire department.

This was not the only pursuit I was in during my time on patrol. One night I was assigned to the west hill district. I was parked under a bank drive up window at Pacific Highway South and Kent Des Moines Road. Another motorcycle went westbound on Kent Des Moines RD running the light at the intersection. I initiated a pursuit and notified the Des Moines Police as we just had entered their jurisdiction. I chased the motorcycle all the way through Des Moines at 70 MPH and entered Normandy Park. I was very familiar with the roads in these jurisdictions as I was still a volunteer firefighter there. I followed the motorcycle for about fifteen minutes in a circle through Normandy Park and finally found him parked in front of his house. Needless to say he was arrested for

Reckless Driving and Eluding a Police Officer.

On another graveyard shift, I was called to a reported house fire on Pacific Highway South at about 250th. My role was to block the highway while the fire department extinguished the fire. I parked in the middle lane with my emergency lights on and watched the action for about 20 minutes. Dispatched then toned out an emergency tone for a Robbery in Progress at 240th and PHS. I attempted to get in my patrol unit only to find that I had locked myself out. I ran down the driveway towards the house fire and told the firefighters that I needed a coat hanger. They looked at me like I was crazy but did retrieve one from the house. I was able to open my car and responded to the Robbery. When I arrived,

I found a lone attendant who told me two white male adults had robbed him at gun point. He had written down the make, model, color, and partial license number of the getaway vehicle on a napkin. As I was transmitting that information and taking a report, I noticed that the attendant had wet himself. He told me that he was scared to death that he would be killed during the robbery. A couple of months later' I received a call from the King County Sheriff's detective division. They said that they had person in custody that knew a lot about the robbery that took place on Kent west hill. I responded to their east side precinct and started to question the suspect. He told me he was the driver of the getaway vehicle in the robbery and told me the name of the robber. I also got a phone log from this suspects mother and did reverse directories on the incoming phone calls. The driver told me the other suspect had gone to Oxnard, California. One of the incoming phone calls was from the Oxnard area and revealed a possible address for the suspect. I requested an arrest warrant for the other suspect and called Oxnard PD. They went to the address and found the vehicle that was used in the Kent robbery. They knocked on the door and entered finding the suspect in a bedroom under the bed with a gun. He was taken into custody and extradited back to Washington State. He stood trial and was convicted of first-degree robbery and sentenced to jail. The Oxnard arresting detective was brought up for the trial and his testimony assisted in the conviction.

Chapter Eight

During my early law enforcement career all officers still carried revolvers. I carried a 357 magnum with a six-inch barrel. I also changed my holster to a clam shell one. The purpose of the clam shell holster was to make sure my weapon was secure. I would have to push the button by the trigger in order to release the weapon from the holster. If I attempted to remove the weapon prior to pushing the button the holster would not activate. Once the button was pushed, the holster would open like a clam and the weapon would be able to be drawn. This operation was very quick and almost silent. I drew that weapon many times during my law enforcement career, but I never had to discharge it in a fire fight. I was extremely fortunate in that aspect. At least three times during my career I could have justifiably shot someone, but the bad guys would back down before I would have to do that.

One afternoon I was assigned to the east hill district. I was in a turn lane following a pick-up truck when I ran the plate for expired tabs. Dispatch responded that the pick-up was associated with a felony subject. I initiated a traffic stop in the parking lot of a Rite Aid store. We were about one hundred feet from the front of the store. I approached very cautiously and got the two occupants identified. It turned out the driver was the one with the felony warrant. Since I was by myself, I decided the situation was very dangerous. I unlocked my shotgun and requested back up. The backup officers were minutes away. I took my shotgun and pointing it at the pickup I yelled for the occupants to put their hands on the dash. I told them not to move or they would be shot. When my back up arrived, we took the suspect into custody without incident. The pickup was impounded, and we had located a handgun under the seat of the truck. After the incident was over, I went to the front of the Rite Aid store and located several witnesses. They told me that when I had yelled at the occupants of the pickup some of them had turned around and placed their hands on the wall of the store. We had a good laugh and they thanked me for my service.

Another time while assigned to the east hill district I was dispatched to a robbery that had just occurred at a local tavern. I responded and started looking for the suspect. We had a good description of him as a white male adult, long dark hair, and a beard. After several minutes we located that suspect and took him into custody. He was booked into the King County Jail in downtown Seattle as he also had a number of warrants out for his arrest. It was my job to take a witness to the jail for a formal identification. We needed five more white males with beards to initiate the lineup. The "pay" for the other inmates was a pack of cigarettes for ten minutes work. We located five other inmates and was getting ready to conduct the lineup. At that time, I realized the robber had shaved off his beard. We had to go back to the jail and find five other inmates without beards. After finding the new inmates we walked them into the lineup room. My witness was on the other side of a one-way glass partition. My witness told me that the robber was number three but that he had shaved his beard. The robber was convicted and sentenced for second degree robbery.

A couple of months later our
administration decided to conduct
undercover operations in the parking
lot of a well-known east hill tavern.
It was widely known that a large
number of drug transactions were
happening in this parking lot on
weekend nights. The administration
obtained a group of officers, some
in plain clothes and several patrol
vehicles with uniformed officers.
We placed an officer on the roof
of the tavern with binoculars and
his role was one of the spotters.
He would watch a transaction go
down and would notify the officers
on the ground. We would make
the arrest and the bad guys would
be transported to jail by the patrol
officers. Each operation would take

as little as ten minutes and once
the patrol officer took the suspect
away, we would start all over again.
Captain Dennis Byerly commanded
this operation. Captain Byerly was
a very athletic and tough individual.
He would never allow his officers to
do anything that he was not ready
to do himself. The spotter on the
roof of the tavern called on the radio
that a drug deal was going down in
a tan van. Captain Byerly was the
closest officer the van and started
to intervene to make the arrest.
The van started to drive away,
and Captain Byerly jumped into
the open passenger side door. He
reached for the driver and turned
off the keys. I was the next closest
officer, (in plain clothes) and was

ready to assist the captain with
the arrest. Out of the corner of my
eye I saw an individual approach
us from behind. This person had a
knife in his hand and came at us in
an aggressive manner. I drew my
weapon and told the suspect to drop
the knife. I also identified myself as
a police officer and ordered him to
stop advancing on us. The suspect
was approximately twenty feet away
when he decided to drop the knife.
I took him into custody, seized
the knife and he was booked into
jail on a misdemeanor charge of
possession of a weapon. During his
misdemeanor trial, after I gave my
testimony, the judge looked at the
suspect and told him he was lucky to
be alive. The judge also told him that

he would have probably shot him,
and he was very lucky that I had not.

Chapter Nine

During my time in patrol the City of Kent had two major fires of suspicious origin and cause. Because I had a fire service background, I was assigned to assist the fire department investigating these fires.

One of these suspicious fires was in a restaurant in downtown Kent in the middle of the night. The fire caused major damage to the structure and appeared like an arson fire to the local fire marshal. I spent several days with the fire marshal, and we located a couple of wax candles on top of a large freezer unit, the knobs to the gas range were in the open position and were missing, and the back door was found to be unlocked. We learned that the initial call of the fire was reported to be of an explosive type, and we noted that the windows were blown out which is typical of a gas fueled fire. Several personal items from the owner were missing also. The owner was interviewed but maintained his innocence. While we were unable to charge the owner with Arson, we turned our information over to his insurance company who decided NOT to pay him for the loss. Sometimes hitting a person in their pocketbook was just as damaging as an Arson charge.

One night the City of Kent had
a large fire at a large apartment
complex at the base of Kent Des
Moines Road. The fire destroyed
the manager's office/apartment
and the community building for the
complex. I was assigned to again
assist the Kent Fire Marshal in the
investigation of this fire. During
the scene examination we located
many bundles of nickel want ads
partially singed from the fire. During
the investigation we learned that
the ex-husband of the manager had
threatened to burn the complex.
We located the ex-husband's
residence at an apartment in the
Sea-Tac area. I located several
more bundles of nickel want ads in
the dumpster next to his residence.

After obtaining a search warrant for the apartment, I spent several hours searching the residence which was located on the second floor of an apartment complex. During the search I observed that the ex-husband was very meticulous in how he stored his clothing and other items. In his hall closet I noticed that his shirts were color coordinated and hung in a very straight manner approximately one inch apart. His shoes were also set in a straight manner. I photographed my findings. While on the floor next to the hall closet, I observed a red spot on the closet track. I pulled up a portion of the rug next to the closet and found a large red spot underneath. It looked to me that some foul play had occurred near the closet. Since my warrant was for Arson evidence, I immediately stopped my search. I contacted the King County Sheriff's detective division because that is whose jurisdiction, I was in. I asked them if they had any open cases associated with the location I was at. They advised me that they had an open homicide investigation from the previous month. Apparently, they had located a female body directly below this apartment's balcony. They also told me that they had located a bloody jacket in a tree above the body. I told them of my findings, and they immediately took action. Using my findings, they obtained an additional search warrant for the ex-husband's apartment. In the apartment they located a sizable portion of blood under the balcony's fake grass covering. They ended up arresting the ex-husband for Murder and he was convicted of that crime.

Chapter Ten

In late 1981 the department decide that
it needed a detective division. A number
of officers applied, and I was chosen as
one of the original six officers to start
the division. My first assignment was

narcotics, and my partner was Larry Wandry. We both grew out our hair and beards. We were also given fake Washington state drivers licenses. My undercover name was Randy David James with my same date of birth. I kept it simple so I would not forget it under pressure. This was a difficult assignment for me, as I had worked hard to be a straight and clean police officer and now, I had to act like a drug dealer. Larry and I decided early on that we would never do hard drugs as part of our assignment. We did get a small quantity of numbing powder used by dentists. When we were pushed to use cocaine by our contacts, we told them we had the best cocaine around and had them sample our "drug." It numbed immediately and always worked to our advantage. During our assignment, we had a number of interesting buys and busts.

Working narcotics, we would always start with a small or medium dealer and attempt to work our way up to greater suspects. This process took many hours of investigative work. We would also use confidential informants to introduce us to the dealers. Once we got to a larger dealer, we would set up a buy and make an arrest. Here are some of our more memorable arrests:

We had developed a lead to buy several hits of acid. Those hits were small squares with different symbols on them that contained the drug. The buy was to occur in a University of Washington apartment in downtown

Seattle. I was the one making the buy. My backup was outside and after I gave the signal that the buy was made, they would come upstairs and make the arrest. When the time came to make the buy, I entered the apartment. It contained four other individuals, and I was pretty nervous. I had left the apartment door partially open when I came in. The dealer presented a Tupperware container that held about twenty-five sheets of acid. I signaled for my backup using a device hidden in a pack of cigarettes. Suddenly, the door to the apartment sucked closed. It sounded like a heard of elephants coming up the stairs. Everyone in the room looked around nervously and I pulled my handgun to control the situation. Just then four persons (from the Seattle Police Narcotics Unit) broke into the apartment and pointed their weapons at me yelling me to drop my weapon. Luckily the next person in the room was my partner, Larry Wandry. He told them that I was the good guy and not to shoot me. All the others were taken into custody and arrested for drug possession and distribution. This operation took a number of hours and we had been out of contact with our dispatch during this time. When we finally got back into our jurisdiction dispatch advised me to contact my residence. I called my wife, and she told me that dispatch had called her two hours earlier to ask about my where abouts. She told them she did not know. She was glad that I was safe. She had been nervous for my wellbeing as being out of contact with dispatch was an unusual situation.

On another buy I was to purchase ten pounds of marijuana. We used a seized undercover vehicle, and I met the dealer in a parking lot in east Kent/Maple Valley. This was the first time we had used the signaling device hidden in a pack of cigarettes. What we did not realize was the foil inside the pack would stop the signal from going out. Luckily, we had a backup signal, me pressing the brake lights on. When the dealer got into my car, he put a large bag into the back seat. I could

smell the marijuana immediately. I
handed the dealer a large bundle
of cash and as he was counting
it while I attempted to signal my
backup team. When I realized the
cigarette pack was not working, I
attempted to push the brake pedal.
I then remembered that I had to
turn on the car for the brake lights
to work. I started the vehicle and
the dealer looked over at me asking
what I was doing. I told him I was
cold. He started to reach under his
jacket (which I later learned he had
a weapon there) and I pulled my
revolver out of my ankle holster. I
stuck my gun into the dealer's ear
and told him to freeze. He asked
me one question. "Is this a bust or
a rip off?" I told him it was a bust

and he told me to produce some police identification. I told him that I did not have any on me as I was undercover. He was instructed to place his hands on the dash and that was when my back up team arrived and took him into custody.

Larry and I spent a lot of time in taverns as that was the place to get to know who the dealers were and attempt to make deals. A couple of times we had to go the station and take breathalyzers in order to determine if we were sober enough to drive home.

During my time in narcotics the state narcotics association was holding a conference in Wenatchee, Washington. Five of us thought it would be a good idea to ride our motorcycles over to the conference. We notified the Washington State Patrol when we would be leaving and the route we were taking (Interstate 90). Once we got on I-90 we noticed a state trooper on the side of the highway. He pulled up next to us and gave us the high sign and then he escorted us for many miles. Once he turned off, we were met with another trooper who continued to escort us for a number of miles. This exchange occurred all the way to the conference. Later that night, I was heading to my motel when I was pulled over by a Wenatchee Police Officer. As he approached, I noticed that he had his hand on his service weapon. He asked me for my driver's license. After I produced it, I told him I was a Kent Police Officer and was here for the conference. He told me I looked nothing like my driver's photo. I produced my undercover license, and he could not believe that both were photos of me. He had stopped me for a taillight out and gave me a verbal warning and sent me on my way.

A couple of weeks later my partner Larry Wandry was making drug purchase at a local tavern. My role was to wait outside in the parking lot to assist in the arrest. I observed my partner and the drug dealer exit the tavern and my partner gave me the signal that the deal had been done. As I approached them my partner was behind the dealer, and he observed the dealer reaching into his jacket. Larry grabbed the dealer from behind in a bear hug. I drew my weapon and pointed it directly at the suspect. I was in front of the suspect with my weapon in his chest. Larry looked at me and shook his head as if I discharged my weapon the bullet would go through the suspect and hit my partner. We told the suspect he was under arrest. The suspect then brought his hand out from the jacket and an automatic firearm dropped to the ground. The suspect was taken into custody and booked into the Kent jail for dealing cocaine.

As I mentioned before we often

went to several taverns in order to attempt to purchase drugs. One Friday night we had been in a tavern and had met a potential dealer. The next day my wife and I were at the Safeway store on Pacific Hwy South when I saw the potential dealer also in the store. I told my wife to play along as we approached this person. I introduced my wife to the dealer as "my old lady" and told him that I would meet him the next week to discuss the purchase of the drugs we had talked about the night before. After leaving the store, my wife told me to not ever introduce her as my old lady. We had a laugh about this and was not ever going to do that again.

Chapter Eleven

In the summer of 1982, the detective division got an all call to the Green River as some kids had observed a body below the green river bridge stuck onto a piling. We responded and along with the help of several officers we located the body of a female person covered with green algae. We photographed the victim and used a tarp to wrap around her and remove her from the river. During this time, many media were present up on the river side. Captain Hal Rees told the media not to show myself or Larry on camera. Both Larry and I were shown on TV that night and that was the end of our undercover operations. Captain Reese called later that night and told me that I would be moving over to Homicide. Little did we know that this female, later identified as Wendy Caulfield was that first victim of Gary Ridgeway, the Green River Killer. (Ridgeway was ultimately arrested in 1998 and confessed to 48 murders of young women. He told investigators that he may have killed at least eighty women but only 48 were found.) It was obvious that Wendy had floated down the river and had gotten lodged on this piling. She was soon identified, and my sergeant and I had the task of notifying her next of kin. We located Wendy's mother in Tacoma and when we identified ourselves all the mother could say was "I knew something bad was going to happen to her." Due to the amount of algae on Wendy's body we had to determine where and how long she had been in the river. I called the University of Washington and spoke with a professor there. When asked the best way to determine where the algae came from, he told me to buy a number of ham hocks with the skin still on them. I placed the ham hocks in four different locations, in the river, south of where Wendy was found and over the next week photographed them twice a day and took notes about the collection of algae on the ham hocks. On day six I noted that one of the ham hocks had accumulated approximately the same amount of algae that was on Wendy's body. That led investigators to believe Wendy had been in the water for about a week and the approximate location where she was placed into the river.

Over the next six weeks, seven more deceased women were located south of Kent either in or on the shores of the Green River. The locations where the bodies were found were in the jurisdiction of the King County Sheriff's office and they took the lead in the investigation. Detective David Reichert was assigned as the lead detective and the Green River Task force was formed. For the rest of the summer, I was assigned along with several other officers to conduct surveillance of the Green River Road from an apartment overlooking the road. We did the surveillance twenty -four seven for about a month taking down license plate numbers and during the day photographing all vehicles that had traveled that road. After that summer, I returned to the detective division in Kent.

We had four homicides during that fall
and into the next year.

Chapter Twelve

In October 1982 I was notified of a possible crime scene on the west hill of Kent on 30th Ave South. I was tasked with investigating the scene. I was assisted with this scene investigation by the Washington State Patrol criminalist section. After obtaining a search warrant, we began our search for clues. We learned that a young female had answered a help want ad for a company called Comp-Tec at this location. Her name was Geri Marie Slough. We located blood splatters on and beside a desk in the main part of the small office area. There was also a desk pad that had some indentation writing on it. The scene was diagramed and photographed. We collected a large number of pieces of evidence and logged them systematically. We learned that the person who rented the office was a man named Charles Schickler. Across from the office we located a mailbox that contained a large number of letters answering the want ad. One of the letters came from the Kent Police Chief's daughter. Over the next week we continued the investigation. We located Schickler's vehicle, after he had run off the road near Alder Lake next to Mt. Rainier National Park. After finding the vehicle at a tow yard we pulled the trunk lock mechanism to make sure that Geri was not there. We impounded the vehicle, and had it towed to our storage yard where we conducted a forensic exam of the vehicle after obtaining a search warrant. Again, I was assisted by a criminalist from the Washington State Crime Lab. We located a large number of blood spots inside the trunk. I diagramed the trunk, and we began collecting evidence. I would take sterile piece of gauze, dip it in a saline solution and after dipping it in the blood spots place it into a small plastic evidence bag. The criminalist had very shaky hands and I would have to mimic his shakes in order for me to drop the samples in. This got to be quite a scene as he continued to shake, and I continued to try and shake the samples in order to place them properly. A couple of days later we were notified that a fisherman on Alder Lake had found the body of a female. The lake is so large that it has its own current. A number of us took up a position east of where the fisherman saw the body and just as it started to get dark Geri's body floated towards the dock I was on. I took a long stick and caught Geri as she was floating by. Geri had a rope tied around her with a small boat anchor attached. She was positively identified by dental records the next day by the King County Medical Examiner's office. She had been shot in the back a number of times and had her breasts removed by a knife. During the next several days we secured a search warrant for Mr. Schickler's residence and boat. We located a similar piece of rope and did not locate any anchors during our search. We learned that Mr. Schickler was in custody in Kitsap County across Puget Sound. He had been arrested for burglarizing a Cub Scout camp and told arresting authorities he was on the run from the Kent Police Department. We were notified and Detective Bob Holt went to the Kitsap County Jail to interview him. Detective Holt spent four hours with Mr. Schickler and was just getting down to the murder of Ms. Slough when a jailer stepped into the interview room to give the prisoner dinner. This interruption caused the conversation to come to a complete halt. As much as Detective Holt tried, he could not get Mr. Schickler to continue with his admission of this crime. A number of days later we learned that Mr. Schickler attempted suicide by hanging himself in the Kitsap jail. He was in a coma for several months and finely died saving the taxpayers a large amount of money for trials, etc.

One Sunday morning I was called to
investigate a possible homicide directly
behind the police headquarters. All
the other detectives were assisting the
Green River Task Force, so I was the
one left to conduct this investigation. I
was accompanied by Police Chief Jay
Skewes. The victim was an elderly male
who had been stomped to death in the
middle of the street. There was a large
amount of blood and bloody footprints
leading away from the body. Chief
Skewes and I followed the footprints
behind an adjacent residence to a small
shed. We located blood on the door
and under it also. Prior to opening the
door, Chief Skewes asked me if I had
any extra ammunition as he had not
loaded his revolver prior to leaving his
home. I gave him my extra ammo. We

knocked on the door and someone inside told us to go away. We opened the door and found a white male inside a sleeping bag with bloody shoes near the door. The suspect also had blood on his hands and on the sleeping bag. We took him into custody and booked him into jail on suspicion of homicide. I processed the arrest scene and took seventeen pieces of evidence. During most homicide investigations we normally collect hundreds of pieces of evidence. In this case I collected seventeen, almost unheard of. We photographed the scene and the deceased. The victim was taken to the medical examiners. During my interview with the suspect, he told me at he was an agent with the CIA (Central Intelligence Agency) I actually called the local office of the CIA and asked them if

this person was an agent. The checked
and told me that he was not an agent
with them. Later when he was on trial, he
acted as his own defense attorney. While
on the stand he attempted to discredit
me and my investigative techniques. He
was unsuccessful in that attempt. This
is the only time in my law enforcement
career when I was the arresting officer,
the crime scene officer, the evidence
officer and investigating officer. Chief
Skewes gave me a one-page document
basically saying that all questions about
this investigation should be brought to my
attention. The suspect was convicted of
second-degree murder and sentenced to
a long stint in prison.

Chapter Thirteen

After twenty months in the detective division, I was rotated back to the patrol division. This was kind of a letdown as I went from investigating narcotics and homicides to answering barking dog complaints. But I shaved my beard and cut my hair and went back. During this time, I encountered a number of interesting situations.

During one afternoon we were notified of a possible kidnap that had occurred on the east hill of Kent from a daycare center. We learned that a white female had taken a child, not her own, from a

daycare and got into a blue cab and left
the area. Our dispatchers did a great job
by calling all the local cab companies to
find out who had blue cabs and which of
those cabs picked up a woman and child
at the daycare. After several minutes
we were told that a cab had done the
pick-up and was headed for Seattle
Tacoma International Airport. They were
currently heading west from the Kent
valley floor to 188th Street. I was the
west hill assignment and was several
miles away on Interstate 5. I proceeded
northbound on I-5 at a high rate of speed
in an attempt to block the cab. I exited at
188th and started down towards the Kent
valley. Several units were coming up
behind the cab and as they pulled the cab
over, I blocked the cab from the front. As
I contacted the driver a number of officers

went to the back door and confronted the suspect. One of the officers took custody of the child as others took custody of the suspect. We later learned that the woman had two plane tickets to Texas and that she had recently been stalking the daycare looking for a child to take. The baby was returned to the daycare and the custody of her real mother. The woman was booked on kidnapping charges.

Late one evening I was assigned to the East hill district. As I was monitoring the radio, I heard Officer Bill Ross telling dispatch that he was located behind the Roadside Tavern when he observed shots fired near the front of the tavern. I responded down James Hill as backup and hit 70 mph as I was heading to officer Ross's location. I took up a position north of the Tavern and learned that officer Ross was doing CPR on the victim. The victim ultimately died at the scene and the suspect was not apprehended.

On another day we were dispatched to a fight in progress at the 7-11 store on Meeker Street. We arrived to find a couple of biker types fighting outside of the store. It took a number of officers to secure one of the bikers. As we took him into custody, I pulled on a chain that was attached to his nose and ear. Needless to say, he went ballistic. We pepper sprayed him in the back of the patrol car. That pepper spray hit a number of the officers also. If you have never been pepper sprayed before you will always remember it. He was finally taken into custody and booked into our jail for disorderly conduct.

One day I was assigned to the downtown district. We were dispatched to a silent bank alarm. I responded and took up a position a block west of the bank. I unlocked my shotgun and began walking towards the bank. The sidewalk had a number of people on it that didn't seem to pay much attention to my presence. As I got closer to the bank, I racked a round in the breach of the gun. That racking noise sent all of the people scrambling into nearby storefronts. When I reached the corner near the bank dispatched informed us that the alarm was false and a bank employee was coming out of the bank's front door. Since you never know if the employee is operating under duress, we had the employee get on his knees and we approached cautiously. It turned out to be a false alarm and the scene was cleared and turned back to the bank.

One of the most difficult tasks that I went through during my law enforcement career was attending police officers' funerals. On June 24th 1982 Detective Sheriff Samuel Hicks was shot down by a homicide suspect in the rural area of east Kent. As Sam and his partner traveled down a long dirt road, the suspect opened fire from the nearby tree line with a high powered rifle. Sam was mortally wounded, and his partner escaped unscathed. A large manhunt was conducted, and the suspect was finally caught several days later hiding in the woods. Detective Hicks was given a full Law Enforcement funeral and attending that funeral left an impact on me that I will never forget.

On March 27th 1984, Detective Michael Raburn was serving an eviction notice in downtown Seattle. After identifying himself he was stabbed by a long sword through an opening in the door. I could not bring myself to attend this Detective's funeral. He too was given a full Law Enforcement funeral.

Chapter Fourteen
Fire Service Career

In 1985 I tested for a fulltime position with King County Fire District #26 in Des Moines, Washington. This was the same department that I had volunteer with since 1976. I was chosen and soon was directed to the Washington State Fire Academy near North Bend, Washington. This was a brand-new facility, and I was part of the first academy class to attend this 8-week training. The director of the academy was a retired Assistant Chief from the Seattle Fire Department. He was a very stern leader and demanded strict attention to the training. This training was very physical and had the recruit's doing firefighting, ladder drills, fire pump evolutions and much more. During one of the rescue drills I was to act as a lost firefighter inside a burning structure. While I did have a self-contained breathing apparatus on, I was lying behind a couch when rescuers were trying to locate me. I was there for an extended period of time and to be honest was starting to run out of air and becoming claustrophobic. Finally, I was located by the only female recruit in the class, and she pulled me to safety. This had an impact on my belief about the ability of females in the fire service. I grew to respect her during the academy. She proved to be just as capable as many of the male recruits. After graduating from the academy, I went back to fire district #26 and began my professional career in the fire service.

I walked into the fire station on my first day and attempted to make coffee for the troops. Of course, I screwed it up and ended up burning up the coffee maker that I soon learned how to rewire. Starting out as a newly hired firefighter was a new challenge for me. I was assigned to tasks that were menial and I was not a very happy employee for the first couple of months. I did make every attempt to do what I was told but it was difficult. While at Des Moines I did have several responses that left an undeletable mark on my life.

King County Fire District #26 Firefighter

One of the main trainings we received was to become Emergency Medical Technicians. Medic One was just beginning in our state and they were tasked in training first aid responders to the higher level of EMTs. All of us below the rank of chief became EMTs after intense training.

We did a lot of Cardio-Pulmonary

Resuscitation during my early years. This was before the do not resuscitate laws and we would attempt CPR on almost every patient who was unresponsive. There were at least four nursing homes in our jurisdiction and CPR was a common occurrence several times a week. We also taught how to use a defibrillator during this time. Automatic defibrillators were not invented yet, so we were using manual defibrillators. Our training cultivated with shocking large dogs who were sedated and whose heart rates were sent into ventricular fibrillation so we could shock the dog back into a normal sinus rhythm. Many of the students walked away from the training as they could not shock an animal.

On one occasion, we were called to

one of our nursing homes with CPR in progress. We took over the CPR from the staff there and I was tasked with setting up the defibrillator. I charged the paddles to 300 joules and just as I told everyone to clear and get ready to shock, the patient opened her eyes and started to breath on her own. We did not shock this patient.

For one week myself and Dave Mataftin were assigned to the Aid Car. Every day we were dispatched to an emergency medical aid. By day four all of our patients had died for one reason or another. On day five we were sent to a young man with a broken leg. By that time, we were feeling low as all of our critical patients that week had passed away. We were wondering if we could save this patient with a broken leg. We did and ended the week with a save.

The 4th of July is notoriously a very busy day with many brush and tree fires. I was assigned to the Aid Car again and was dispatched to a possible childbirth. When we arrived, we found the mother sitting on the toilet and she had given birth into the toilet. We had to retrieve the infant who was obviously deceased. This was a very traumatic incident for me, and I struggled with this for a long period of time.

Des Moines fire had a resident program where volunteers could live in that fire station and respond when they were available. On Valentine's Day many of the residents were not "at home" and the morning after we got a call of an apartment fire on Kent-Des Moines Road.

I was the only paid firefighter on duty and had two residents available. As I was driving the fire engine out of the station, I observed a large column of smoke coming from the area of the apartment. I directed my residents to "mask up". When we got closer to the apartment fire, I saw that we had a six unit building with fire pouring out of the ground floor middle apartment. I called for assistance and ordered my residents to pull a large 2 ½ inch hose line and attempt to extinguish the fire. (I had learned early in my career "large fire equals large water" I engaged the pump as they began attacking the fire. I instinctively knew that the hose line they had and the amount of fire they encountered would soon deplete the tank water that I had in the pumper. I then connected to a nearby fire hydrant and started to supply them with that water. My residents were able to knock down the bulk of the fire while other help arrived. I learned later that two occupants were exiting the front of the apartment as we were attacking the fire from the rear. Those occupants were extremely lucky to have escaped the fire when they did. The fire was mopped up and we cleared the scene several hours later.

Late one night we were called to a commercial structure fire at the local Safeway store on Pacific Hwy South. When we arrived, we found that the wooden pallets stacked behind the store were fully involved with fire. It took us an hour and a half to extinguish that fire and pull down the pallets in order to make sure the fire was completely out. Luckily the fire did not breach to back wall of the store and the inside was left undamaged.

One afternoon, while assigned to the Aid Car, we were dispatched to a car-pedestrian accident near Highline Community College. After arriving we found a ten-year-old boy under the front end of a vehicle. The boy had been dragged face down by this vehicle for a number of feet. He had lost most of his skin on the front of his body and was in extreme pain. We extricated him from under the car and provided first aid until Medic One arrived and took over the boy's care.

Late on Prom night we were dispatched to a single vehicle accident at South 240th and Marine View Drive. Upon arrival, we located a car about one-hundred feet

up on the lawn of Judson Park. The car
had failed to negotiate the curve in the
road there and launched itself over the
rockery there. While others attended to
the driver, I went to the passenger side.
I located a female, dressed in a beautiful
blue dress, scrunched into the passenger
side under the dashboard. I extricated the
female and found she was not breathing
and had no pulse. We began CPR and
the only injuries that were obvious was
a small cut below her chin. I used that
cut to lift her chin so I could properly
administer oxygen while others did chest
compressions. I will never forget the look
of this patient while we attempted to save
her life. It turned out she was severally
damaged throughout her body from the
extreme speed and sudden crash of the
vehicle. She was not wearing a seatbelt

at the time of the crash. The driver was not seriously injured and smelled of intoxicants. He was ultimately arrested for vehicular homicide. This was one of my most tragic emergency scenes during my time at Des Moines.

It was common for only one professional firefighter to be on shift at a time. This was usually overnight or on weekends. One weekend late afternoon I was dispatched to a kitchen fire in our neighboring jurisdiction which we served. I responded by myself and made sure dispatch was aware of this. I got to the scene and observed smoke coming from the open front door. I exited the fire engine and engaged the pump. I then pulled a hundred- and fifty-foot section of 1 ½ inch hose line to the front door of the residence. By the time I had this laid out several other members arrived and quickly extinguished the fire.

One of the best parts of working for Des Moines is our jurisdiction had a jet powered fire boat. This was the only fire boat between Seattle and Tacoma. During the summer months we would conduct simulated water rescues and other close quarter maneuvers. It was not uncommon to spend several hours a day out on the fire boat. The power for this boat was jet propulsion that sucked water under the boat up and exiting it to the bow and stern of the boat. It was a little tricky moving the boat from side to side and one would have to use several levers to accomplish this. We also had to attend a number of Coast Guard classes in order to become a pilot for this boat.

One Saturday afternoon, I was out on the boat alone. I was south of the Des Moines marina moving around several buoys. All of a sudden, the boat lost power and I came to realize that I had sucked up a large amount of seaweed into the pump. This had happened before, so I knew that I had to shut the boat down, open the engine hatch and dig the seaweed out to clear the engine. As I was attempting this action, I found that the tide had pushed me into the shore. I became stuck and felt very foolish. I got on the radio and contacted the fire station on a seldom used radio channel. The last thing I needed was the media to find out that I had run aground in this very expensive piece of equipment. After several attempts, someone answered my radio call and soon several firefighters came to my rescue. They were able to push me off the beach and I luckily made it back to the marina without any more incidents. All in all, this was the best summer ever learning to properly use this boat.

During my time at Des Moines, I had the opportunity to go back to the fire academy as an instructor. I believe that I was one of the first firefighters to be a recruit and then return as an instructor. I oversaw physical fitness training and ladder evolutions. This time at the academy allowed me to work hard to ensure that every member of the recruit class was successful in their time there.

Washington State Training Academy

While at Des Moines the department
hired a few new firefighters. So, I wasn't
the rookie for very long. This allowed
me to pursue other interests in the fire
service. I began instructing first aid and
CPR training to the public along with new
volunteer firefighters. I also started to gain
interest in fire prevention. I was allowed

to work on a computer program in order to make fire prevention inspections easier for the firefighters. Remember this was in the early times for computers so all I had was a word processor that I had to manipulate so the result was a clear word document for us to use.

I attended additional training in Port Orchard one weekend and a portion of the training had to do with a new study on the effects of trauma on emergency responders. The instructor provided a list of possible symptoms for Post-Traumatic Stress. Looking over that list I realized that I had several the symptoms. During this time, we were told not to complain about what we saw or did. So, I secretly went to a therapist in Tacoma and was able to "dump my trashcan" of emotions and come to understand why I felt the way I did. These therapy sessions helped me deal with the traumatic scenes that I had been subject to early in my career.

Chapter Fifteen
Salem Fire Department

In January 1987, our first son was born. We named him Joshua Ray Johnson. In early 1988 we sold our home and moved to Salem, Oregon.

I had applied for the Salem Oregon Fire Department as a Deputy Fire Marshal. The department was hiring two DFM's and I scored number one and was hired. Working for Salem had its good times and it bad. Mostly good times though. We first moved to the small adjacent community of Keizer, Oregon. I started attending Chemeketa Community College taking courses in Fire Prevention/Insurance

Risk. During this time, I contacted the Washington Adoptees Rights Movement in an attempt to find my birth mother. I paid the $300 fee for the search and about three weeks later we were informed that WARM had found my original birth certificate and made contact with my birth mother. Their rules were to give the birth mother three opportunities to turn down their request. My mom did want to find me and reached out one night while I was away at night school. When I returned home, I learned that my wife had spoken to my birth mother and that she was coming to Keizer the next weekend

Salem Deputy
Fire Marshal

to meet me. This meeting was the single most life changing event for me and my family. The next Saturday my mom and stepfather arrived at our home. After the initial embrace, she told me that she would have to teach me to HUG. We had a good laugh about that. They stayed all of Saturday and most of Sunday before heading for home which was just outside of Tacoma, Washington in the small-town Orting. With her she took several family photographs that we had given her. When she returned home, she attempted to put the pictures away but couldn't get the box open to do so. One of her daughters, my half-sister, asked her who the photos were of. My mom told her about me and my family in Oregon. My half-sister called me that night and we began a lifelong bond. My birth mother was one of nine children in her family. Several weeks later my wife, son and I went to Orting where we were greeted by a large contingent of relatives. I called this my coming out party. In 1990 our second son was born. We named him Christopher Joe Johnson. His middle name is my stepfathers first name.

During my ten years at the Salem Fire Department, I took advantage of numerous training opportunities. I attended the National Fire Academy in Emmitsburg, Maryland several times and also Western State College earning both a Fire Administrative Institute Certification along with an Advanced Fire Administrative Certificate. Both of these required me to attend six-week

courses in fire administration
laws and techniques. I also
received an associate degree from
Chemeketa Community College in
fire prevention/insurance risk. The
director of this program asked me to
develop several of the courses as
they had not been done yet. I also
tested for and received an I.C.B.O.
certified plans examiner and certified
Uniform code inspector.

During the early years at Salem,
I met with other fire marshals like
Ron Smith from Marion County Fire.
Together we formed the Marion/
Polk fire investigation team. At the
peak of our existence, we had 52
members of the team from both
counties. We met monthly along with

the Marion County District Attorney
and several law enforcement
members. If any jurisdiction had a
major fire or a fatality fire members
of the team were called to assist in
the investigations. At one point I was
nominated as the president of the
team. The team members worked
together on a number of fires.

One day as I was returning from my
classes, I was notified of a large fire
in Downtown Salem. I responded
and was assigned as the primary
investigator. The fire started in a
local restaurant when the cook
flipped a hamburger and the fire
from the grill ignited the overhead
grease trap. The fire then extended
upwards and due to the degrading

of the flue the fire then moved
horizontally through the ceiling area.
The ceiling was made of copper
and the firefighters inside could not
breach the ceiling. The fire exploded
out of the front of the restaurant's
front doorway. This fire burned
for several hours and destroyed
several businesses adjacent to the
restaurant. It was stopped along the
south at a gas station and along the
north by a three-story commercial
building. I requested Fire Marshal
Smith to go to a twelve-story
building on the next block and obtain
photographs from the roof of that
building. The fire occurred at noon
time and at least ten vehicles were
located in front of the block. Those
ten vehicles were also damaged

by this fire. Firefighters stayed at the scene through the night extinguishing hot spots. I returned to the scene the next day. The restaurant had collapsed on itself and had been mostly extinguished. In order to verify the cause of the fire I had to climb through the collapsed building. I was attached to a rope and made my way to the kitchen debris. I made observations and photographed my findings. With an automatic camera I was able to shoot upwards in the flue and verify that a large amount of grease was there. This buildup of grease was determined to be the likely cause of this fire. It took me several days to finish the investigation reports.

One night we were called to a
multiple fatality fire just east of the
downtown area. I requested several
team members, the Salem Police
Department and the prosecutor's
office to the scene. We set up a
command post and began our
investigation. Two of the victims were
transported to the hospital and one
victim was deceased at the scene.
The scene was a multi-unit older
home and the main fire had occurred
in the basement apartment. While
law enforcement was interviewing
witnesses, I was tasked to diagram
the scene and the apartment
where one of the victims still laid.
I spent several hours measuring
and sketching the scene including
the final position of the victim. It

was deathly quiet while I was doing this. At approximately 5:30 a.m. I was just completing my diagrams when a clock radio came on with loud music. It scared the day lights out of me. During the course of the investigation, we learned the two Molotov cocktails had been thrown through the basement windows and ignited the contents of the room. The two victims who went to the hospital passed away along with the victim at the scene. We were able to collect glass shards from the devices and secured them as evidence. All the victims were African American and through investigation techniques we learned that the suspects were white. Fire Marshal Smith and I conducted several tests to determine how the

Molotov cocktails acted when thrown through the windows. Three suspects were brought to trial and two of them were found guilty of multiple murder. This investigation was truly a team effort and solidified that using a team process was very successful in the prosecution of the suspects.

About midnight one night I was called to assist in the investigation of a fatality fire at the base of Orchard Heights Road in west Salem. When I arrived, that first thing I saw was three blue tarps on the ground in front of the residence. Under those tarps were three children who had died in the fire. The children were 3, 5 and 8. Right after I arrived, a woman came running up screaming and I learned that this woman was the mother of the children. She had apparently been out for the evening and had just returned home. The surviving child was a 12-year-old boy. the mother had told him to clean the fireplace while she was out. He put the fireplace ashes into a paper sack and placed the sack onto the back porch of the house. This older home was made of balloon construction, meaning that there was limited fire stops in the construction of the structure. The disposed ashes were fanned by winds and the paper sack caught fire and extended upwards to the second floor and entered the structure from a window there. The twelve-year-old was downstairs watching television and did not realize that the second floor was on fire until it was too late. The three children died in their beds from smoke inhalation. There were smoke alarms in the house but none of them had working batteries in them. This was another of the most devastating incidents that I was involved in during my career. At a later time, the Salem Fire Department along with the local Kiwanis club and the Home Depot put together a smoke alarm program to give away 9-volt batteries and smoke alarms to anyone who needed them. One of those free smoke alarms saved a family in west Salem later that year.

One night I was dispatched to a residential fire/explosion. When I arrived, the fire had already been knocked down. I observed that large portions of the home had been blown outwards. This included the front door and most of the windows. Both items were mostly intact and lying several feet from the residence. I learned that two victims had been in the home at the time of the explosion. The female victim had been in the kitchen area under a countertop pasting wall paper. The debris from the explosion blew past her and out the rear sliding glass door. She escaped through the sliding door cutting her feet on the broken glass. During the investigation I learned that the Director of the Oregon State Bomb Squad lived nearby. I asked him to

look at the scene and give me an
idea of what had occurred. He told
me that it looked like a natural gas
explosion. I located the gas meter
near where the front door had been
and shut off the gas supply. For the
first hour of the investigation, we
could not locate that male victim.
After removing debris from a large
hole near the front door we located
the male victim. He was impaled into
the furnace located in the basement.
Crews recovered the victim, and
I continued the investigation. I
interviewed the female victim, and
we then secured the scene. The
next morning, I returned to continue.
I made my way into the basement
and then to a small shop area near
the furnace. I noticed that there

was a crack in the basement wall near where the gas supply line entered the home. I also saw a desk lamp with the switch in the on position. I photographed and diagramed the scene. I contacted the natural gas company and asked for an investigator from them. They provided several people, and the gas meter was secured for later forensic analysis. It should be noted that natural gas is odorless on its own. An additional gas is added that smells like rotten eggs. This is called mercaptan. During the next several days I interviewed the female victim several times. I learned that she was an insurance agent and that she had several life insurance policies on her husband. This was an interesting twist in the investigation, however I excluded her as having anything to do with the fire/explosion. A week later I attended the testing of the gas meter and during the testing learned that the meter was working as it should. I did learn that several months prior to this incident Salem had a minor earthquake. I surmised that this earthquake caused a leak in the neighborhood's gas supply line. The gas followed the path of least resistance and the mercaptan smell was screened from the natural gas and entered that home through the crack in the basement wall. The husband, not knowing that a flammable gas was present, turned on that light or some other ignition source causing the explosion/

fire. I later took my investigation materials to a Denver Colorado Fire Investigation Conference and discussed my findings with several well-known investigators. They came to the same conclusion as I did.

During my time at Salem the fire investigation team we had formed was called out to several large fires in both Marion and Polk counties. We found that using team resources was an affective and efficient way to conduct an investigation.

As I explained before I took advantage of every training opportunity that I could while at Salem. One of those opportunities that presented itself was attending that Western State College campus to complete an Advance Fire Administrative Institute Certification. During this training, I met one of the instructors several times. He was the Assistant Chief of Training for the New York City Fire Department. As he and I were having lunch one day he invited me to New York to speak to a new Arson Investigators class and ride along with the fire department. Several months later, after attending the National Fire Academy, I got a ride to New York City by one of the other students in attendance. When I arrived at Randall's Island the site of the FDNY fire academy. I was greeted by a training Captain in a bunk room. He offered me a beer and opened a commercial ice chest and got me one. We then went fishing on an adjacent dock along the Hudson River. He was my personnel escort during the four days I was there. We went to the top of the World Trade Center and visited several unique areas around the City. On Sunday I was driven to one of the oldest fire stations in the city. I rode with the Battalion Chief and his driver. We didn't go on many calls however it was an experience that I won't soon forget. On that Monday morning I was asked to be that guest speaker to a large class of newly promoted fire investigators. I spoke for about 30 minutes discussing our local fire investigation team and how it worked. Later that day I was picked up by two fire investigators. The first thing that they did was issue me a bullet proof vest. After putting it on I was in the back seat of the patrol vehicle and one of them asked me if I knew how to shoot a gun. I told them I did, and he opened the center console and pointed to a firearm there. He said that if we were in a firefight that weapon was the one, I was to use. Needless to say I was a little overwhelmed, however I took it all in stride and rode with them for several hours. We investigated two fires that day and the later dropped me back to the fire academy. The captain drove me to the airport the next day and I flew home with a ton of new experiences.

Late one evening I was called to

investigate a commercial structure fire. The industry was a wood working plant and was well involved when fire crews arrived. The metal building was energized with electricity and crews could not add water to the fire until the electricity was turned off. Once the fire was extinguished, I began my investigation. It turned out the company used linseed oil as part of their process. I located a metal trash container near the area of origin and in the container was several rags soaked with linseed oil. When linseed oil is combined with cotton rags it will spontaneously combust. This turned out to be the cause of this fire.

One afternoon I was called to investigate a fire in a garage and attached residential home. During the course of this investigation, I learned that the homeowner was working on a vehicle in the garage and attempting to remove a fuel pump from the gas tank. The homeowner was emptying the gas tank into several five-gallon buckets and had spilled a portion of gas onto the garage floor. The fumes from the gas traveled along the floor and was ignited by a pilot light from the nearby furnace. The homeowner saw the ignited gas coming towards him and ran out of the open garage door after catching on fire. Two children were in the home at the time of the fire and escaped through the rear sliding glass door. They had just learned what to do in case of a fire the week before from a public ed class at their school.

One of my most interesting investigations was a commercial structure fire in the afternoon. It had been reported that a propane tank had caught fire and blew up. The tank had exploded and ended up a block away from the fire scene. During the investigation I learned that the propane tank was being removed from a vehicle in a shop area. The propane tank rolled off a pallet and propane gas, which is heavier than air, traveled along the shop floor and was ignited by a wood stove several feet away. Luckily no one was injured as a result of this fire.

Chapter Sixteen

In late 1995 I tested for the Fire Marshal's position in Salem. I came out number one and was promoted by Fire Chief Jim Bone. During my time as the Fire Marshal/Division

Salem Fire Division Chief

Chief I was appointed by Governor Kitzhaber to the states Local Emergency Planning Committee. This committee oversaw all of the emergency planning throughout the state of Oregon. I also was asked to speak to the State Senate on residential fire sprinklers. I oversaw the fire prevention division with five deputy fire marshals. One of those fire marshals was new to the Salem Fire Department. He was a difficult employee and weekly I would get complaints about his demeanor and attitude while doing his job. I would counsel him weekly and try to calm him down. Because he was on probation, I ended up letting him go from employment. It was a difficult decision for me, but I had documented his actions and had plenty of reasons to end his employment. While I was the Fire Marshal Chief Bone retired. The City of Salem hired a new fire chief by the name of Casey Jones. Chief Jones and I didn't see eye to eye very often and at the end of my probation he demoted me back to a Deputy Fire Marshal position. This action was devastating for me as I had worked very hard to get to where I was with the department. It turned out that all the Division Chiefs either were demoted or left the department during Chief Jones tenure. The only saving grace for me was I was assigned to oversee a multi-million-dollar project for Mitsubishi Silicon American which was building a semiconductor plant in south Salem. It was not uncommon for me to spend four out of five days at the plant looking over plans and designs in this new industry. The Uniform Fire Code hadn't even caught up with this industry and a lot of the procedures and new technology had to be thought through and I made sure that the plant was built as safely as possible. Many new techniques were tested and sometimes

I would have to approve the design of these new procedures as we went along. On one occasion a very large tank of hydrogen was filled in the cool of the morning and as the day heated up the tank released a large volume of gas into the atmosphere. I had to call the fire department's hazardous materials response team to make sure the release of this flammable gas was done safely. The release took a couple of hours and luckily no catastrophes occurred. One of the other processes used Silane gas. Silane gas was so volatile that if the gas came into contact with oxygen, it would spontaneously explode. The bunker that the gas was housed in had an explosive roof structure that if the gas did denotate the blast would go upwards as opposed to outwards. The bunker was protected

with Aqueous Film Forming Foam
(AFFF). The foam was activated using
heat detectors and was very costly to
test. The company did not want to test
this system due to the cost, however, I
convinced them that it was vital to the
safeguard of the bunker that we needed
to do an actual test of the activation of the
foam used to protect the bunker. During
the final phase of the plant, the company
had a party and myself and Chief Jones
attended. I was
singled out by the
CEO of Mitsubishi
Silicon America
for my efforts in
assisting with the
completion of the
project.

Salem Fire Marshal

Chapter Seventeen

A couple of months later I was interviewed by the regional director of a Country wide company who conducted private fire investigations and was hired by them. As a fire investigator I was assigned to the southern portion of Washington state and the whole of the state of Oregon. We worked for a number of insurance adjusters and when they had a suspicious or large loss fire, we would be hired to investigate the origin and cause of those fires. In August of 1998, I studied for and received a State of Oregon Licensed Private Investigators certification. It was not uncommon to investigate three or four fires a week. During my spare time, which wasn't much, I would do fire sprinkler plan reviews for a private firm near me.

On one occasion I was dispatched to a small village north of the Arctic Circle in Alaska to investigate a structure fire that had occurred there. The home that had burned was one of seven homes built there as part of a government project. When I arrived the next day, I learned that the home was destroyed and was nothing but a pile of ash. Luckily all the other homes were constructed the same as the one lost. I used one of the other homes as a template for my investigation. This is the only fire in my career that did not have any suppression efforts during its destruction. All the appliances and other items in the home where laying directly where they were at the time of the fire. After interviewing the occupant of the home, I learned that he had come home late at night intoxicated. He entered the "mud" room and hung up his coat behind a chest freezer. He went on to say that when he awoke later that night the bulk of the fire was coming from the front of the home and mud room. As I was conducting my scene examination, I located the remnants of the jacket behind the freezer and wrapped around the motor there. Later that evening, when I returned to Anchorage the builder took me out to dinner. Leaving the restaurant,

I was blessed to see my first glimpse of the northern lights. It was a sight that I had not seen before and over the years was lucky to see again. This began my love affair with Alaska.

One of the fires that I was dispatched to was outside of Portland, Oregon. The fire occurred on a houseboat on the Columbia River. When I arrived, I noted that a pile of debris was located in the parking lot adjacent to the river. During my scene exam I observed that the Portland Fire Bureau had removed all the items from a bedroom in the structure. This included the wall boards, the bed, the dresser and the carpet. I photographed what was left and then moved to the outside of the houseboat. Near the bedroom window I located a piece of the bed frame with a control mechanism attached. It turned out the bed was a waterbed, and the control mechanism was the heat control for the bed. I learned during my investigation that the female occupant of this room was asleep at the time of the fire. She had laid her pillow on top of the heat control and the pillow caught fire. She awoke to her hair on fire and left immediately. I took the device with me for further forensic analysis. I went back to the parking lot where I reconstructed the bed frame and noted that the missing piece matched her description of the fire. I diagramed and photographed the fire scene and submitted my report to the insurance company. It turned out that the heat mechanism was built in China and the later court case was assigned to the US District Court. I testified, after being Court Certified as an Expert Witness. The forensic engineer could not positively say that the heating device, due to the damage, was the cause of the fire and the defendant company was found not at fault for the fire.

Like I said before, I investigated a large number of fires while employed by this firm. I traveled throughout Oregon, Idaho, Washington and the one case in Alaska. I worked for this firm for approximately one year and found that it did not pay enough to support my family. One day I was at the Salem Library and noticed a book of jobs that included an announcement for the City of Redding, California.

Chapter Eighteen
Redding Fire Department

In the summer of 1999, I tested for an Assistant Fire Marshal position for the City of Redding. I came out number one and was hired. We moved to Redding, and I began my career with them. I attended classes at Shasta Community College and received my Peace Officers Certification from them.

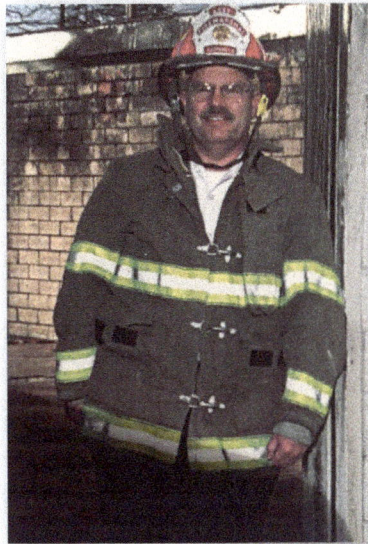

Redding Fire Investigator

The first few years at Redding my primary duties included plan reviews and inspections of new and remodeled properties. I also participated in fire investigations, and it was common for me to be the lead investigator due to my background. Some of the new construction projects that I was involved in were a new Lowes Hardware Store, a large museum, the Sundial Bridge project and many other smaller projects. I was assisted with these projects by fire inspector Dean Herzberg. I am sorry to say that Dean passed away in 2015 from work related cancer. He was a great investigator and a good friend.

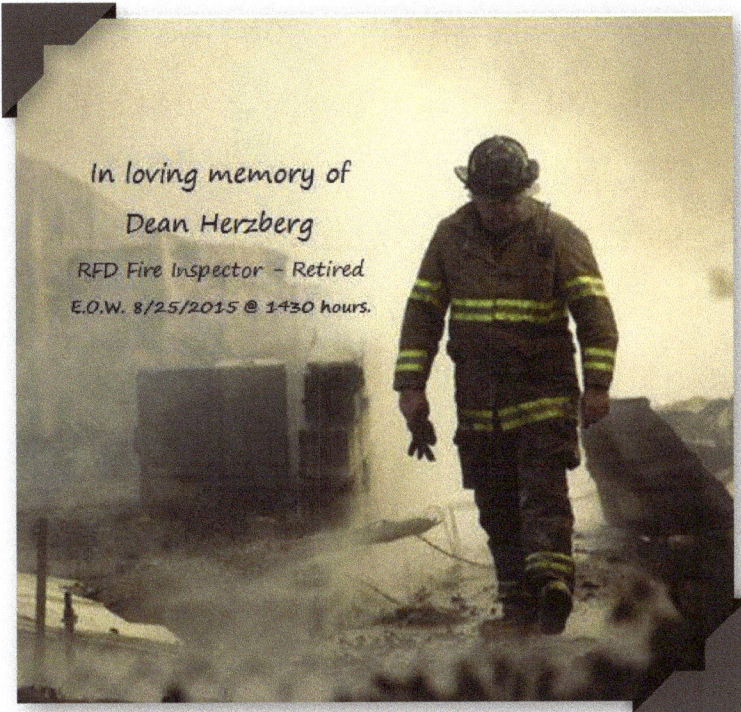

In loving memory of
Dean Herzberg
RFD Fire Inspector - Retired
E.O.W. 8/25/2015 @ 1430 hours.

Dean Herzberg Memorial

While at Redding I continued my
education. I received a Bachelor's
Degree in Business and Human
Resource Management from
Simpson University. This college
is a Christian facility and several of
my courses were directed towards
that. Since the City was funding my

Classes, they sometimes had an issue with the Christian Courses that I had to take for my degree. I also attended the National Fire Academy and in 2004 and 2006, I was an adjunct instructor for them. I tested for the Deputy Chief/Fire Marshal position while early in my career at Redding, however I did not score high enough to obtain that position.

I was also assigned as one of the Public Information Officers for the fire department. I trained with the California Department of Fire and would often respond to major vegetation fires to assist as a PIO.

The first major fire I was assigned to was the Shasta Fire that started on a motorcycle trail near Shasta

Lake. The fire grew rapidly and was moving Southerly by strong winds destroying about 300 structures before the wind stopped blowing south and the fire was halted at the Sacramento River next to Anderson, CA. A Cal Fire spokesperson and I had to go on the six AM local news station and provide updates on the location, evacuations and progression of the fire. We also had to give updates on the five PM news. We did this for three days straight. On Wednesday after the fire, I attended a Kiwanis club meeting, which I was a member of, and when I entered I was given a standing ovation from the other members of the club. During the highlight of the fire, it moved along the Redding airport. My wife could see it and my family evacuated to the Anderson High school for the night. I slept in our home and didn't get much sleep that night.

One time while I was attending the National Fire Academy a fire broke out in our Redding neighborhood. This fire was caused by a metal blade weed eater that had struck a rock sparking the fire. The wind was blowing, and the humidity was less than 10%. My family wasn't allowed to go home for several hours until the fire was brought under control. I was able to google the location of the fire and shared it with the class I was teaching on the following Monday morning.

The largest single structure fire that
I investigated was a hotel under
construction. The call came in
on the 4th of July and was called
in by a local fast-food worker
as he was arriving to work. The
building was well-involved when
fire crews arrived. There was also
an emergency helicopter in the air
and the crew was able to provide
me with progressive photos as the
fire advanced. As I was responding
from south Redding, I could see the
fire from several miles away. This
is the only fire that I responded to
with lights and siren. Due to the
loss being over five million dollars,
I made a call for assistance from
the Alcohol Tobacco and Firearms
(ATF) national response team. They

arrived and we took co-leadership roles during the investigation. They also provided an accelerant sniffing canine from Spokane Washington. The hotel was under construction and was about 50% completed at the time of the fire. We investigated the fire for several days and determined that it was human caused. The only original suspect lead was a witness who said a Pakistani looking male in a Mercedes was parked nearby at the time of the fire. We were unable to locate the initial suspect. During the course of the investigation, we learned that several Pakistani individuals had visited the site just days before the fire. We developed a timeline and name list associated with this fire. The name "Patel" came up during our investigation, however we were unable to find this person. The construction company had insurance and I spent numerous hours speaking to them concerning this fire loss. A month later they received a five-million-dollar check, and I was assigned to deliver that check to the construction company. The fire remains unsolved.

During my time at Redding, I responded to numerous vegetation fires. Over the course of two years, Redding, Shasta Lake and unincorporated Shasta County had several vegetation fires. The bulk of these fires were always started on south facing slopes of grass along freeway onramps or along highways. After several of these fires were investigated, we determined that the cause was contributed to match/cigarette devices. We collected several of these devices during the course of our investigations. The three jurisdictions formed a task force to aid and compare the cause of these fires. It was suspected that the person starting these fires was either a current or past member of the fire service. We looked over a number of persons and located a volunteer from Shasta Lake who had been let go the year before. This person's red pickup truck was seen at many of the fire scenes. We obtained a search warrant for attaching a tracking device to the pickup. After tracking that person's truck, we determined that he was always near or close by the origins of the fires. An additional search warrant and arrest warrant were obtained, and the suspects' vehicle was searched. Investigators located several match books and packs of cigarettes inside the vehicle in the passenger side door panel. After interviewing the suspect, we learned that he had his son throwing the devices in the locations the father had directed him to. The suspect was charged with several counts of Arson and spent time in prison.

While at Redding, I was in contact with a local Alarm company a lot during my duties. The manager of the Alarm company and I collaborated and provided classes on the City's closed circuit television channel to the firefighters of the city. These classes provided advanced fire alarm information for line inspectors to properly conduct fire prevention inspections for businesses that had alarm systems.

Like I said before, I participated in several vegetation fire investigations. I took several classes on determining the origin and cause of these fires. These classes were intense, but they did strengthen my ability to properly investigate these types of fires.

In 2005, I was promoted to Battalion Chief/Assistant Fire Marshal. While this promotion didn't change my duties much, it did allow me to get overtime for after-hours work. I was fortunate to have a response vehicle that I was allowed to drive home at night and to work in the morning. Both of my sons attended a Christian High School, and I would often drive my youngest son to school before work. My youngest found a set of handcuffs in my center console and handcuffed himself to the grab bar in my truck. As we got closer to the school he began to panic and asked me if I had a handcuff key. I told him I didn't. I drove up to the front of the school and several of his peers were standing outside. They had a good laugh at his expense while I un-cuffed him. Needless to say, he never cuffed himself after that.

Redding Asst. Fire Marshal Plaque

Early one morning the Fire
Department received a fire alarm call
at an east side lumber and hardware

store. When crews arrived, they found fire on the back of the store that had lumber stored there. The crews extinguished the fire, and I was called to investigate. Due to the large amount of lumber, it was difficult to find the origin of the fire. I contacted my friend at the fire alarm company, and he provided a schematic of the building and location of the detection devices. We were able to track the progression of the fire by determining which devices activated first, second and third. Once I located the beginning of the fire, I was not able to locate a source of accidental ignition. This led me to conclude that the fire was intentionally set. No witnesses or suspects could be located.

Redding Fire

Chapter Nineteen

During the last couple years of my career in Redding I began to get burned out by the large amount of work that I had assigned to me. These last two years were my 30th and 31st years in the fire service. I began to get ill and had trouble concentrating on my work. Luckily, I had accumulated a large amount of sick leave. I took advantage of the sick leave and sought out medical attention to determine what was wrong with me. When it was all said and done, I retired on a disability retirement in 2007. One of the reasons I retired was one of the fire departments favorite Captains had died from a heart attack while I was on leave. I went to his open casket viewing and attended his funeral services and determined that I did not want to go out that way. Shortly after my retirement my wife of 27 years left me and we filed for a divorce. The divorce was not an amiable one and our attorneys went after everything they could. She won out in the long run.

Chapter Twenty

Shortly after separating from my wife, I moved to McConnellsburg, PA to be closer to the National Fire Academy. I also was hired to convert an International Code Council book to adapt it to include the appropriate California Codes. The trip across the country took me eleven days as I visited several vacation spots along the way. Once I was in McConnellsburg, I found a second story apartment above an insurance company. My adjunct instructor's role ended, and I was left with not much to do. I made friends with Harvey Kneas at a local church, and he was instrumental in keeping me from losing it. I volunteered at the town library several days a week and attended church. My friend Ron Biesold kept in contact with me while I was in McConnellsburg. He visited me once while I was there and ultimately convinced me to come back to the west coast as that is where my sons were. He flew back to PA and along with some friends we loaded up a U-Haul and put my car on a flatbed trailer. He was in a hurry to get home and we made it back to Washington State in three- and one-half days. He had found me an apartment in Enumclaw, WA near where he lived. I began working for the Pierce County Library system and did that for a couple of years. I then was hired by the St. Elizabeth hospital as a security officer. After a couple of years, I tested and was promoted to Lead Security

Officer for the hospital. I left in 2020 after falling on the helipad during a snowstorm. I injured my back and received a concussion. I later became a Security Officer for Oatridge Security Group out of Tacoma, WA. I finely retired for good in 2022. My career had many ups and downs but mostly I had a very satisfying career. I now live in Auburn, Washington with my girlfriend Carol. We have a very enjoyable life and I keep busy with honey do lists. I hope you enjoyed this book and look forward to your feedback at reddingfireman@gmail.com.

9-11 Never Forget

www.ingramcontent.com/pod-product-compliance
Lightning Source LLC
Chambersburg PA
CBHW051219150426
42812CB00053BA/2523